SHREK THE THIRD

DreamWorks

Popcorn ELT Readers

Meet ... everyone from SHREK THE THIRD

Donkey and **Puss In Boots** are Shrek's friends.

Prince Charming wants to be King of Far Far Away.

Shrek and **Princess Fiona** are ogres.

Arthur is heir to the King's throne.

- Puss In Boots
- Shrek
- Princess Fiona
- Arthur
- Donkey
- Prince Charming

Frog King

Queen

The King and Queen of Far Far Away are Fiona's mother and father. The King is a frog now.

The Fairy Tale Characters

Some of the fairy tale characters are good. They help Shrek.

The fairy tale princesses are friends with Princess Fiona.

Some of the fairy tale characters are bad. They are the villains.

Before you read ...
Who do you like from this story?

New Words

What do these new words mean? Ask your teacher or use your dictionary.

die

The King **died**.

castle

This is a **castle**.

fire

She likes sitting next to the **fire**.

crash

The car **crashed** into a bus.

heir

The King's child was his **heir**.

hurt

The girl's foot **hurts**.

ship

They went on a **ship**.

land

Some animals live on the **land** and some live in the sea.

show

Everyone loved the **show**.

'No way!'

No way!

magic / magician

This is a magician. He does **magic**.

Verbs

Present	Past
break	broke
get off	got off

SHREK THE THIRD

CHAPTER ONE
'I want to be King!'

Prince Charming was a handsome man but he was horrible!

'I want to be King of Far Far Away,' he thought.

But he needed help to be King. So he went to see some fairy tale villains. They weren't nice people! They didn't like Prince Charming.

'My friends, listen to me!' said Prince Charming to the fairy tale villains.

'What do you want? We're not your friends!' they all shouted.

But Prince Charming needed their help. He had an idea!

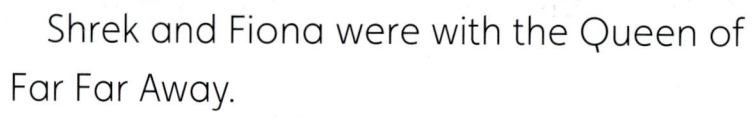

Shrek and Fiona were with the Queen of Far Far Away.

'The King is not well,' the Queen said to them. 'You two must do the King's work.'

So they did the King's work. Shrek was not good at it!

Shrek had to wear the King's shirt and trousers. 'I don't like this, Fiona,' he said.

Shrek started a fire in the castle.

'Oh no, Shrek!' said Fiona.

'Sorry,' said Shrek.

Shrek and Fiona went to see the King. 'I'm dying,' the King said.

Fiona started to cry.

'Shrek, can you be the new King?' asked the King.

'Oh no!' thought Shrek. 'Ogres aren't good kings!' he said. 'Do you have an heir?'

'Yes. His name's Arthur,' said the King and then he died.

CHAPTER TWO
The next heir

The Queen and Fiona were very sad.

Shrek talked to his friends, Donkey and Puss In Boots. 'We must find Arthur,' he said. 'He's going to be King of Far Far Away.'

So the three friends went to find Arthur.

'Bye!' shouted Shrek from the ship.

'You're going to be a father, Shrek!' shouted Fiona.

'A father!' thought Shrek.

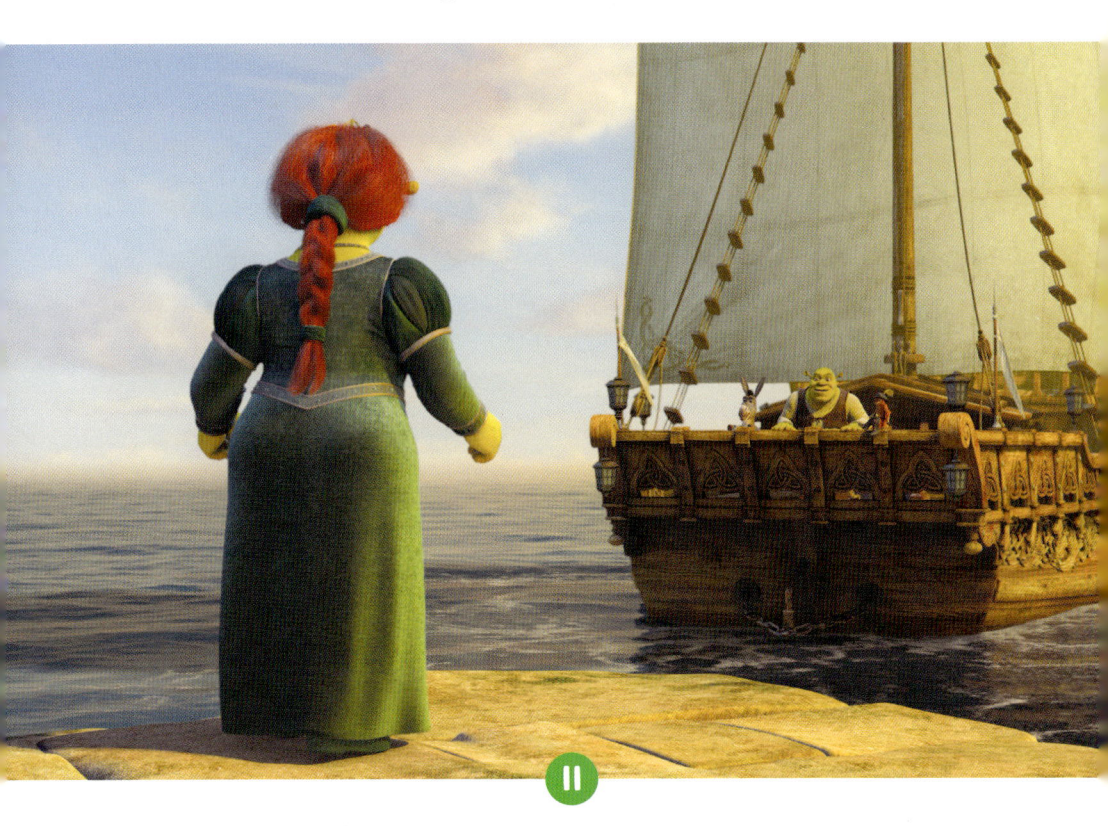

'Don't be frightened,' said Donkey to Shrek. 'I love my children and I'm a good father. You're going to be a great father too, Shrek!'

But Shrek was frightened.

'Me? A father? No way!' he thought.

At the same time, in Far Far Away, Prince Charming talked to the villains.

'No one understands us,' he said. 'The good fairy tale characters have the best of everything. Is that OK?'

'No!' they all shouted.

'Then come with me,' said Prince Charming. 'We're going to Far Far Away!'

'Yes!' they all shouted.

In Far Far Away, the villains broke things and people were very frightened.

'Let's go to the castle!' shouted Prince Charming.

At the castle, Princess Fiona was with her friends – the princesses, Dragon and the fairy tale characters.

Suddenly, the friends stopped talking.

BANG!

Prince Charming and the fairy tale villains were inside the castle.

BANG!

'You go!' said the fairy tale characters to Fiona. 'We're going to stop them.'

'Quick!' said Princess Fiona to the princesses. 'Let's go!'

Prince Charming and the fairy tale villains ran in.

'I am the new King of Far Far Away!' shouted Prince Charming. 'Where are Shrek and Fiona?'

No one said anything.

'WHERE ARE THEY?' shouted Prince Charming to Pinocchio.

Pinocchio was very frightened. 'Shrek went to find the heir to Far Far Away,' he said.

'The next heir,' said Prince Charming. 'We must find him!'

CHAPTER THREE
It's magic!

Shrek, Donkey and Puss In Boots were at sea. They saw a school.

'Stop the ship,' shouted Shrek.

They got off the ship and walked into the school.

'I think that Arthur is a school boy!' said Shrek.

They found Arthur.

'Arthur, you are the King's heir,' said Shrek. 'Come to Far Far Away.'

'Me, a king!' said Arthur. 'Wow!'

They jumped on the ship with Arthur.
BANG!
Arthur crashed the ship. The ship had water in it. They went onto the land.

They saw an old man. He was Merlin the magician!

'Please help us!' said Arthur. 'Please do your magic. We must go to Far Far Away.'

'I don't know. I don't do much magic now,' said Merlin.

Arthur started crying. 'Please!' he said.

Suddenly, there was a 'BANG!' and a 'CRASH!'

Shrek, Donkey, Puss In Boots and Arthur were in Far Far Away! 'Wow!' they said.

Fiona, the Queen and the princesses were outside the castle.

'What's Prince Charming doing? We must find out,' said Fiona.

'I know! Quick! Let's go into the castle!' said Rapunzel.

They went after her and there was Prince Charming. Rapunzel ran into his arms.

'This is the new Queen of Far Far Away,' said Prince Charming.

'Shrek is coming back!' shouted Fiona.

'Good,' said Prince Charming, 'but first you're all going to prison!'

Now in Far Far Away there were villains everywhere.

'This is horrible!' said Shrek.

They found Pinocchio.

'Where's Fiona?' asked Shrek.

'She's in prison. Help her!' said Pinocchio. 'There's going to be a show and Prince Charming is going to hurt you.'

"Oh no!" said Shrek.

CHAPTER FOUR
The horrible show!

Prince Charming thought about the show. He was very happy. 'No more Shrek!' he said with a horrible laugh.

Shrek, Donkey, Puss In Boots and Arthur found Prince Charming inside the castle.

'Where's Fiona?' shouted Shrek.

'Oh good, Shrek! You're here! And here's the new King – Arthur! Ha ha!' Prince Charming laughed. His face was close to Arthur's. 'I'M going to be King.'

'No, stop!' Shrek shouted. 'He's not the heir. I am, OK?'

Arthur looked at him. 'But you said …'

'I didn't want to be King. I had to find someone. And I found you,' Shrek said.

'OK, then,' said Prince Charming. 'Arthur, you can go.'

So Arthur went. He was very sad. 'Shrek never liked me,' he thought.

The fairy tale villains put Donkey and Puss In Boots in prison with Fiona and the princesses.

'Donkey! Puss! Where's Shrek?' asked Fiona.

'Prince Charming's going to kill him in his show,' Donkey said sadly.

The Queen was very angry. She was very strong when she was angry. 'I can break the prison,' she said. And she did it!

'Wow!' said Donkey.

'Let's help Shrek!' said Fiona.

Everyone ran out of the prison.

Prince Charming and the villains started the show. Shrek was very sad.

Fiona, the princesses, Donkey, Puss In Boots and the fairy tale characters ran to the castle.

Suddenly, Donkey saw Arthur. 'Don't go!' shouted Donkey. 'Prince Charming wanted to hurt you. Shrek helped you!'

'I'm coming with you!' Arthur said.

At the show, things were bad for Shrek. His friends wanted to help but it wasn't easy.

Suddenly, Arthur shouted, 'Stop the show! You don't have to be villains. Look at Prince Charming. He's horrible and he's never happy! Do you want to be like him?'

'No!' said the villains.

'Wait! Don't listen to him. I'm the King!' shouted Prince Charming.

'No,' said the villains. 'Arthur is our King.'

'Ar-thur! Ar-thur!' everyone shouted. They were very happy with the new King.

Shrek and Fiona were happy again too!

'Arthur is going to be a great king,' said Shrek.

'And you're going to be a great father,' said Fiona.

THE END

Real World

JOURNEYS BY SEA

Do you like travelling by sea? We look at journeys by sea from a long time ago until now.

8200 - 7600 BC

People used boats a long time ago. First they made boats from trees. They made short journeys in these boats.

boat

1550 - 1600

People made bigger boats. They made ships with sails and three or four masts. Sir Frances Drake, Vasco Da Gama and Christopher Columbus used these ships. They made journeys to look for new places.

mast

sail

1818 – 1970

Then people stopped using sails on ships. Ships had engines. They were bigger and faster. From 1818 ships went over the Atlantic. People travelled between New York and Liverpool.

The Titanic was a famous ship. It started sailing from Liverpool to New York in April 1912. It crashed into an iceberg. Many people died.

The Titanic

Today

Today some people like holidays on a ship. This is a 'cruise'. Cruise ships are very big. A journey on a cruise ship can be short or long.

Would you like to go on a cruise? Where would you like to go?

What do these words mean? Find out.
use   journey   engine   iceberg   holidays

After you read

1 True (✓) or False (✗)? Write in the box.

a) Prince Charming wanted Shrek to be King. ✗
b) The villains were nice people. ☐
c) Shrek didn't like being King. ☐
d) The King had an heir. ☐
e) Donkey has children. ☐
f) Snow White helped Prince Charming. ☐

2 Match the questions and answers.

a) Where did Shrek find Arthur? ii
b) Did the villains help Prince Charming? ☐
c) Who can do magic? ☐
d) How did Shrek go over the sea? ☐
e) What frightens Shrek? ☐
f) What happened to Fiona's dad? ☐

i) By ship.
ii) In the school.
iii) He is going to be a father.
iv) He died.
v) Yes, they did.
vi) Merlin can.

Where's the popcorn?
Look in your book. Can you find it?

Puzzle time!

1 Write the words in the crossword.

Across

2) Shrek is going to die in Prince Charming's horrible ....
3) The magician used ....
4) The ship has .... in it.
5) Shrek thought: 'Me? A father? ....' (2 words)

Down

1) Arthur was King of ....
2) They went over the water in a ....
3) Who can do magic? ....

2a How tall are Shrek and his friends? Match the characters with their heights.

~~Gingerbread Man~~   Shrek   Donkey   Fiona   Puss in Boots

tallest

2.06 metres

1.75 metres

1 metre

75 centimetres

Gingerbread Man   10 centimetres

smallest

b How tall are you? ....

3 Who is it? Match the description with the picture.

i) He's green. He isn't well. He is a frog.

ii) He has long hair. He's handsome. He is horrible.

iii) She's green. She's an ogre. She loves Shrek. She has long hair.

iv) She isn't a good friend. She loves Prince Charming.

Chant

1 Listen and read.

Who am I?

I'm Fiona.
I am green.
I'm an ogre,
Not the Queen!

I am Shrek.
I am frightening!
I don't want
To be the King!

I am Arthur
From over the sea.
I'm the heir,
The King – that's me!

I'm Prince Charming.
I had a show.
When Shrek came along,
I had to go!

2 Say the chant.

Imagine...

1 Choose your favourite character from Shrek.

Shrek

Merlin

Can you ...

walk like him / her?

say 'Hello' like him / her?

sing like him / her?

eat like him / her?

read a book like him / her?

Princess Fiona

Donkey

Prince Charming

2 Work in pairs. Choose a character and an action. Tell your partner what to do. Take turns.

Run like Donkey!

Sing like Shrek.